This eternal thing of people asking me, wouldn't I like to paint all the time, wouldn't I like to do sculpture all the time—it's nonsense. It's not me. Has Condé Nast prevented me from doing good work? I don't think so. Maybe if I'd given up Condé Nast my work would have been worse. I don't think it would be better. And as I learned a long time ago, the life of the artist is quite horrible. There is no success in art. I always felt that life was more important, and that if I had to make the choice I would drop art to save Tatiana, any day. I have absolutely no regrets of any kind.

Alexander Liberman

ALEXANDER LIBERMAN

No Regrets

25 March – 24 April 2004

AMERINGER
YOHE
FINE ART

20 West 57th Street New York, New York 10019
tel: 212 445 0051 fax: 212 445 0102 nycgallery@ameringer-yohe.com

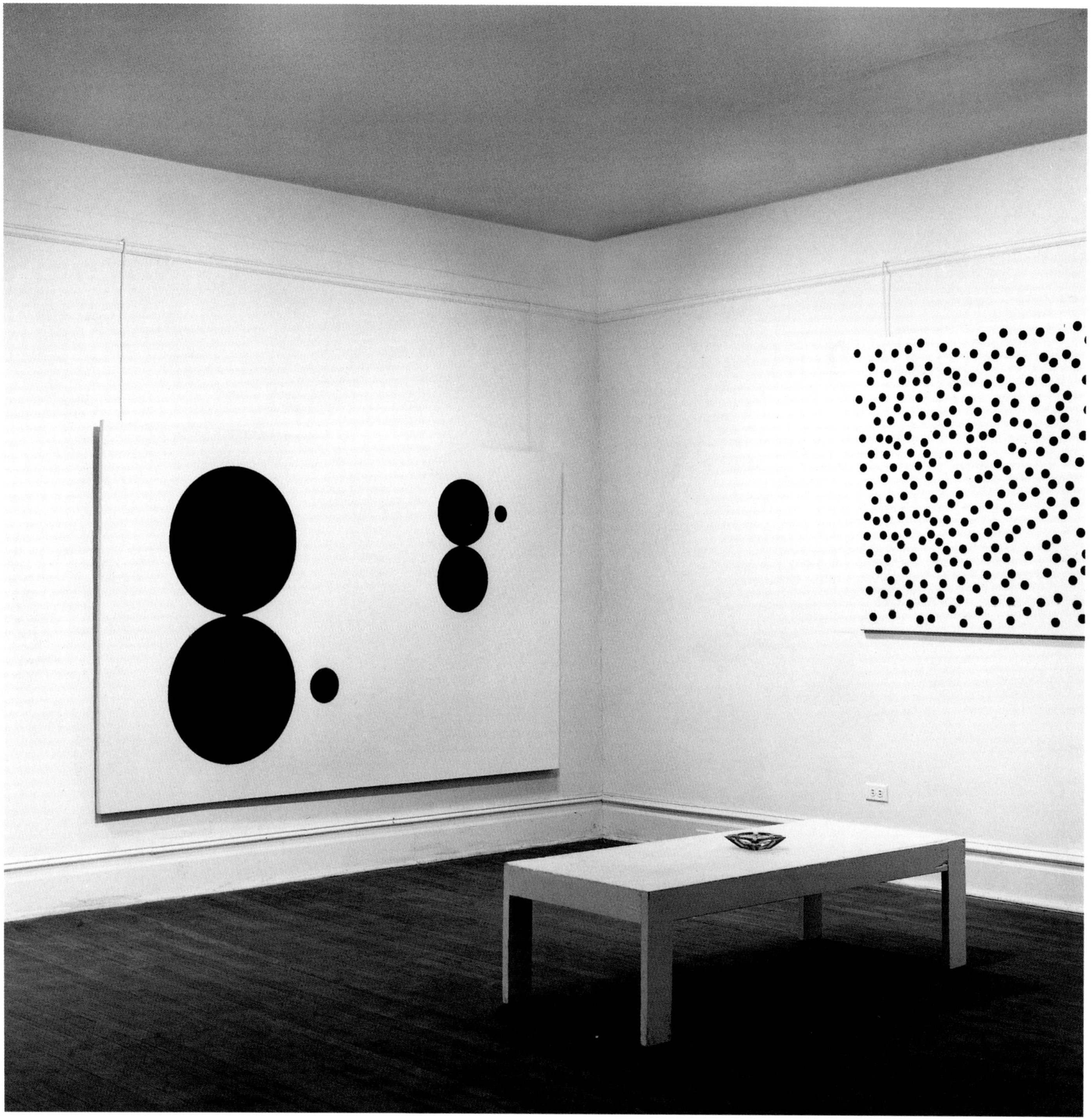

An installation photograph from Alexander Liberman's first exhibition at the Betty Parsons Gallery, April 1960.

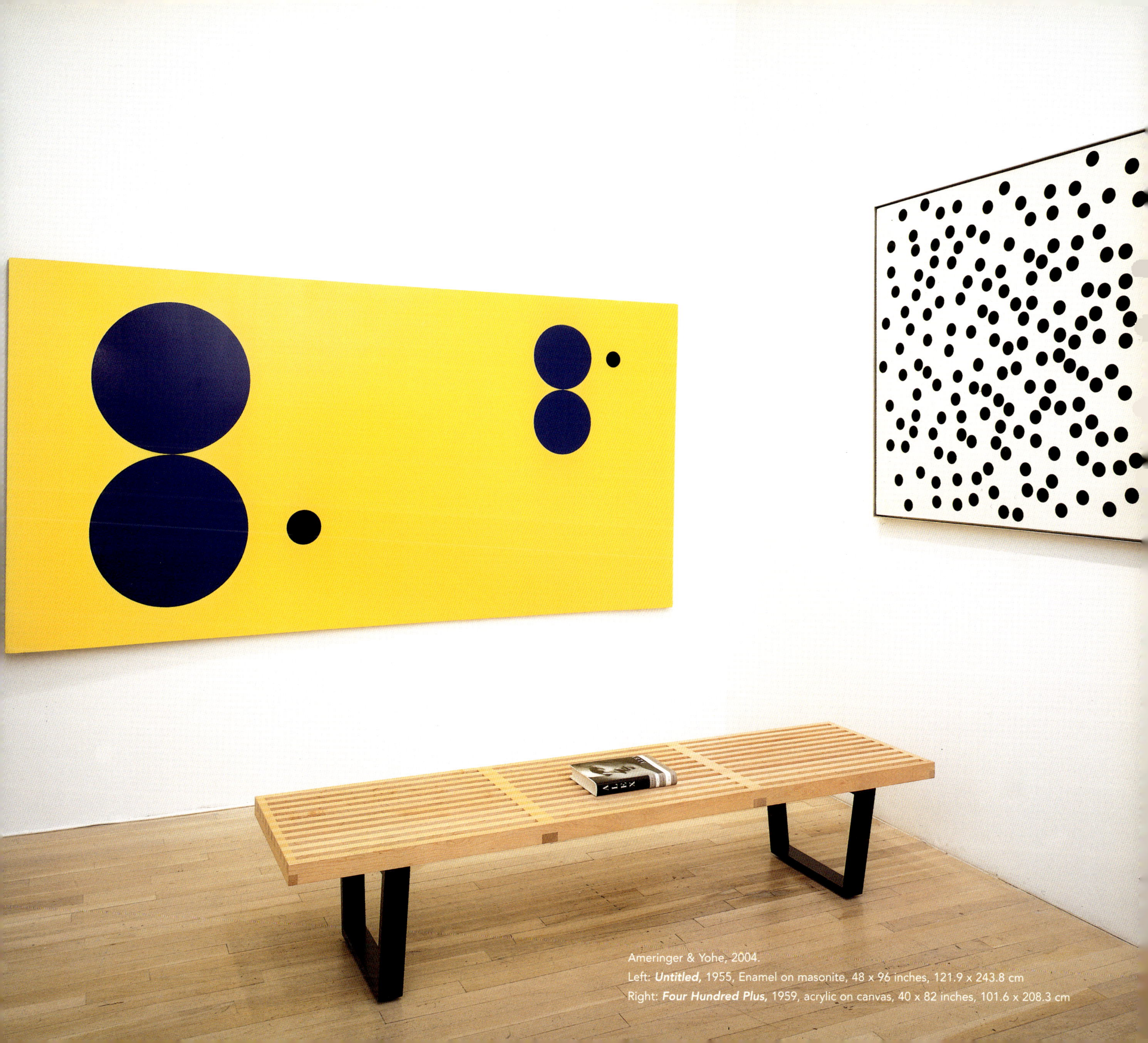

Ameringer & Yohe, 2004.
Left: ***Untitled,*** 1955, Enamel on masonite, 48 x 96 inches, 121.9 x 243.8 cm
Right: ***Four Hundred Plus,*** 1959, acrylic on canvas, 40 x 82 inches, 101.6 x 208.3 cm

His was a life played out against a grand and glamorous background. What begins as an epic refugee tale moving across war-torn Europe becomes a classic American success story in its second act.

The story of Alexander Liberman is the stuff of movies. In fact, after reading Dodie Kazanjian's and Calvin Tomkins' detailed and richly textured account of his life (*Alex: The Life of Alexander Liberman*, Knopf, 1993), cited herein, Liberman suggested Tom Cruise could play a young Alex. But any script would be hard pressed to convey the complicated professional double life he led. Liberman needed to be something of an actor himself to pull it off.

Born into a luxurious yet bohemian Russian family in 1912, he was soon sent off alone to safety, first in England and later in France. There he was always the outsider trying to fit in at the most proper schools and families. His gracious manner and style eased him through each new situation but gave him little personal comfort. There would always be a longing for his lost childhood of security, luxury and art.

Torn between a passion for the arts and the practical reality of survival, as a young man he pursued interests in painting, architecture, advertising, and finally journalism in rapid succession. The consistent element in all of his pursuits was a refined and intellectual aesthetic standard, whether applied to a magazine layout or an abstract painting. He saw no distinction between the endeavors, as the purpose would determine the outcome and the standard would remain the same.

Living in the cafe society of Condé Nast's New York since 1941, he spent the work week remaking our perception of a fashion magazine – "the nobility of *Vogue's* civilizing mission" he called it. On weekends he secreted himself to the studio. Over a period of thirteen years he compulsively painted over two hundred circle compositions. He needed both: the stimulation and financial security of journalism as well as the contemplative life of the artist. Each fed the other literally and figuratively.

It was at *Vogue* that he first emerged into the art world, not as an artist but as a patron. He commissioned Duchamp as early as 1942 to design a cover for the magazine (scandalously rejected as "not right for *Vogue*" and ultimately acquired by the Musée National d'Art Moderne in Paris). He introduced a new kind of photography to fashion journalism, most notably in the work of Irving Penn. In 1951 he had Cecil Beaton photograph models in front of Jackson Pollock's monumental *Lavender Mist* and *Autumn Rhythm*.

Liberman the artist slowly emerges. With the encouragement of Irving Penn, he published his own photo essays of artists' studios in *Vogue*. The collected photographs were chosen by William Lieberman and "The Artist in His Studio" opened at the Museum of Modern Art in November 1959. To even this, Alex Liberman brought his other life. He enlarged, cropped, arranged the exhibition as if it were a magazine layout (see p. 52-53). The exhibition was a huge critical and popular success and led to the first exhibition of Liberman's circle paintings.

Alex Liberman had intimated to Bill Lieberman that Betty Parsons was "interested" in his paintings. In preparing the museum's press release for the photography show, Bill Lieberman asked Parsons about the planned dates for the painting show. "He really pinned her down," said Liberman.

The suggestion was not totally unfounded. Betty Parsons is as legendary as the artists she chose to exhibit. Her gallery was devoted to showing the work of the first generation of Abstract Expressionists, a mission she inherited when Peggy Guggenheim closed her gallery in 1947. The Betty Parsons Gallery, not incidentally, was the setting for Cecil Beaton's confluence of art (Jackson Pollock) and fashion (*Vogue*) commissioned by Liberman.

Barnett Newman, one of Parsons' gallery artists, had brought his dealer to Liberman's studio in 1953. Clement Greenberg was along for the visit. Although nothing happened until the call from the Museum of Modern Art in 1959, Greenberg later pronounced, "Continue with this, Alex, and I will write about you."

Another important studio visit occurred the following year. James Johnson Sweeney went to Alex's studio in 1954 and chose *Two Circles* for his Guggenheim exhibition, "Younger American Painters." The visit and Alex's response again indicate the intertwined relationship between Alex the artist and Alex the editorial director;

"Sweeney came to my studio and chose a painting called Two Circles, *which I had done in 1950. It was two black circles side by side on a white ground — a picture that I happened to*

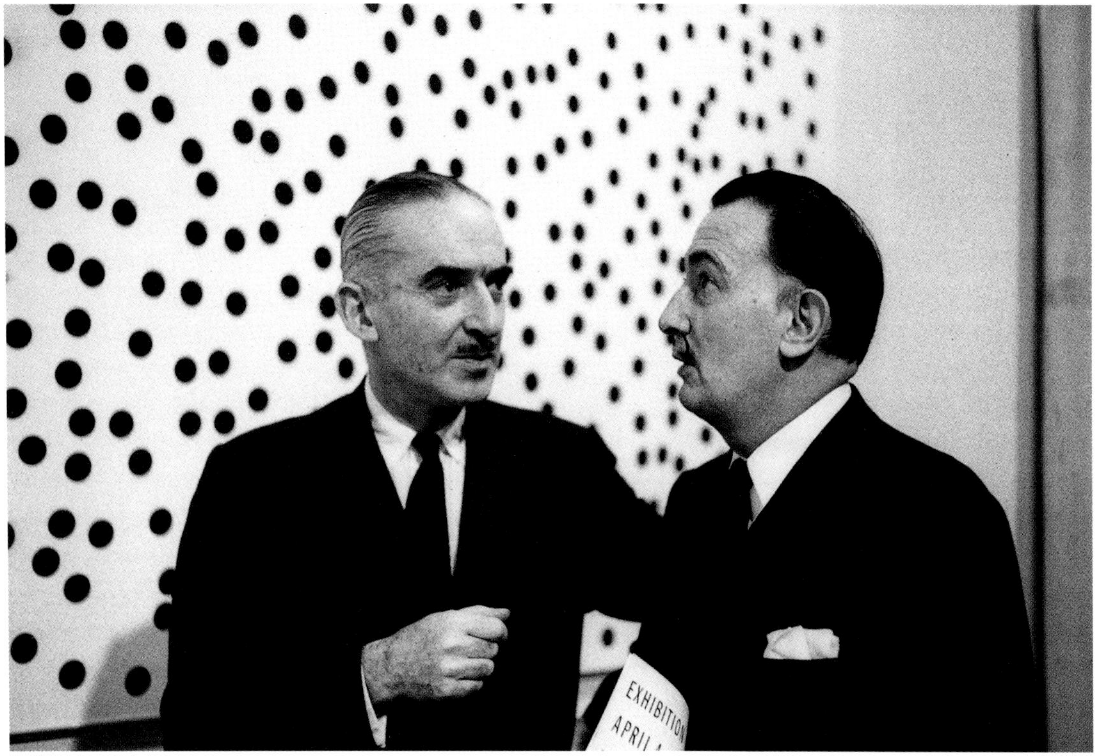

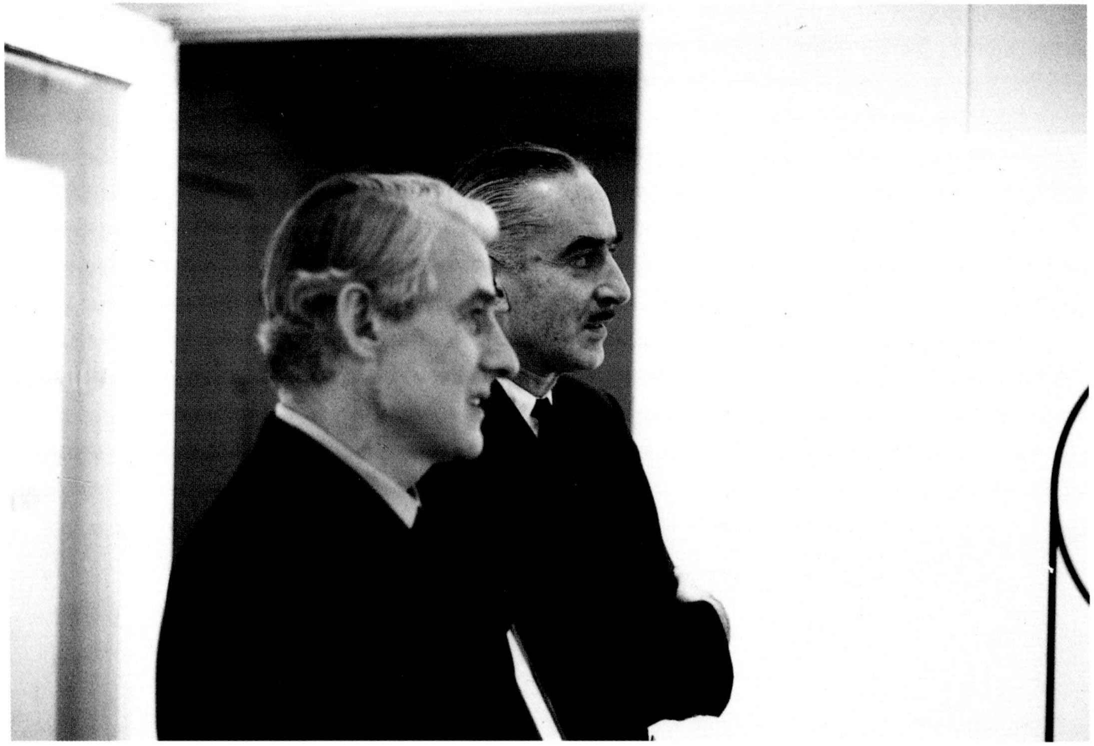

Alexander Liberman at the opening of his 1960
Betty Parsons Gallery exhibition with Salvador Dalí (top),
Willem de Kooning (bottom)...

have executed myself. At least, I had painted the circles with black enamel, on a white background prepared by Eddie Kasper. I had used Du Pont's Duco enamel paint, thinking it would last forever – that was when I had total faith in the products of American technology; I knew nothing about built-in obsolescence – and the white background had turned to ivory in the three years since it had been painted. I asked Sweeney how soon he needed the picture. He said he needed it by the middle of next week and I said, 'Good, I'll make a new one for you.' Sweeney nearly fainted. 'No, no, no', he said, 'I want that one.' So I didn't repaint it, although it would have been much better if I had. My whole theory was that these pictures were repeatable and renewable."

Walter Hopps observed, "In the 1950s Liberman's art was virtually alone in America by employing impersonal techniques with industrial materials." *Two Circles*, now in the collection of the Metropolitan Museum of Art, was the last painting Liberman publicly exhibited until 1960. In light of Liberman's technique and fondness for quoting Pascal's *"Le moi est haïssable"* ("the self is hateful"), it is not surprising that Jasper Johns and Robert Rauchenberg admired *Two Circles* while shown at the Guggenheim. It is also not surprising that Liberman would attempt to recruit the young artists to work for *Vogue*.

Liberman's first one man show opened in April 1960 at the Betty Parsons Gallery. Liberman designed the announcement for the exhibition (p.54), but this time Barnett Newman installed the paintings. Only one painting sold. *Continuous on Red* was chosen by legendary ex-director Alfred Barr for the Museum of Modern Art and was later featured in William Seitz's *Responsive Eye*, the influential 1965 MoMA exhibition. Ellsworth Kelly and Frank Stella admired the painting and wanted to trade their own paintings with Liberman.

Frank Stella's dictum, "what you see is what's there" would belatedly seem to summarize Liberman's circle paintings. That the first of these paintings was executed in 1949 (*Minimum*, also in the collection of the Museum of Modern Art) indicates Liberman's anticipation of many of the ideas and techniques of Minimalism. Barbara Rose, in her 1981 monograph, stresses Liberman's "deepest roots and affinities with transcendental thought in art from eastern Europe," most specifically that of Russian Constructivism, Kandinsky, Malevich, Kupka, and the anonymous artists of the Russian Icons. Liberman himself wrote, "But above all the circle is the purest symbol because it is visible in its totality instantly." From the old world of his Russian youth to the high gloss of American commercial industry, Liberman had come full circle.

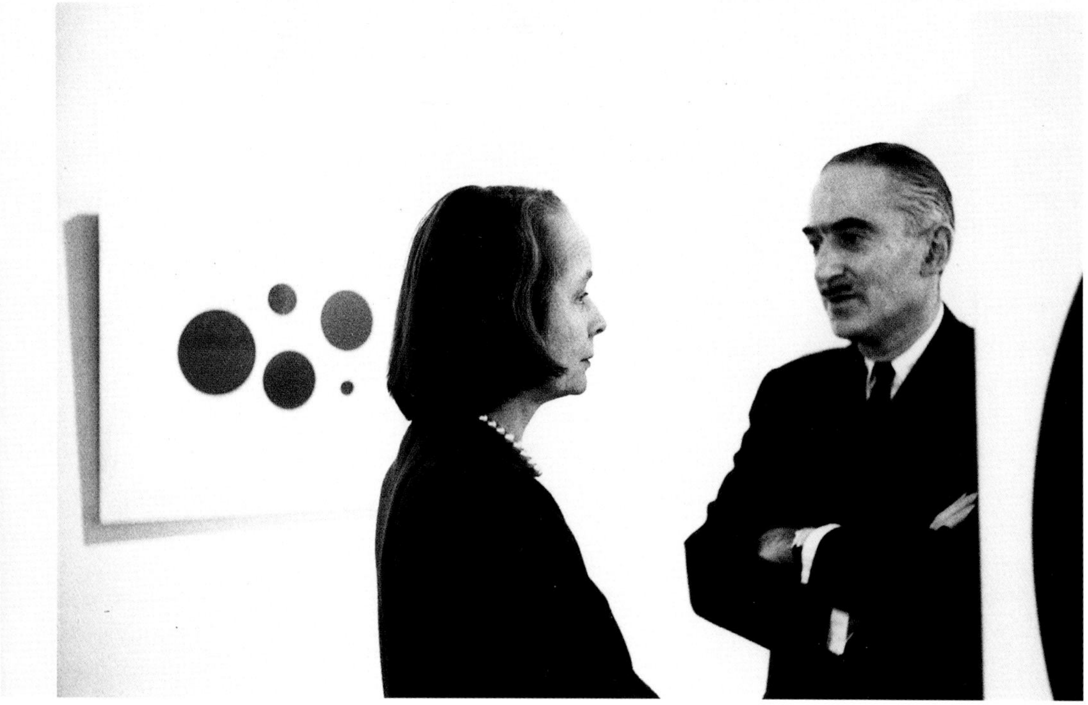

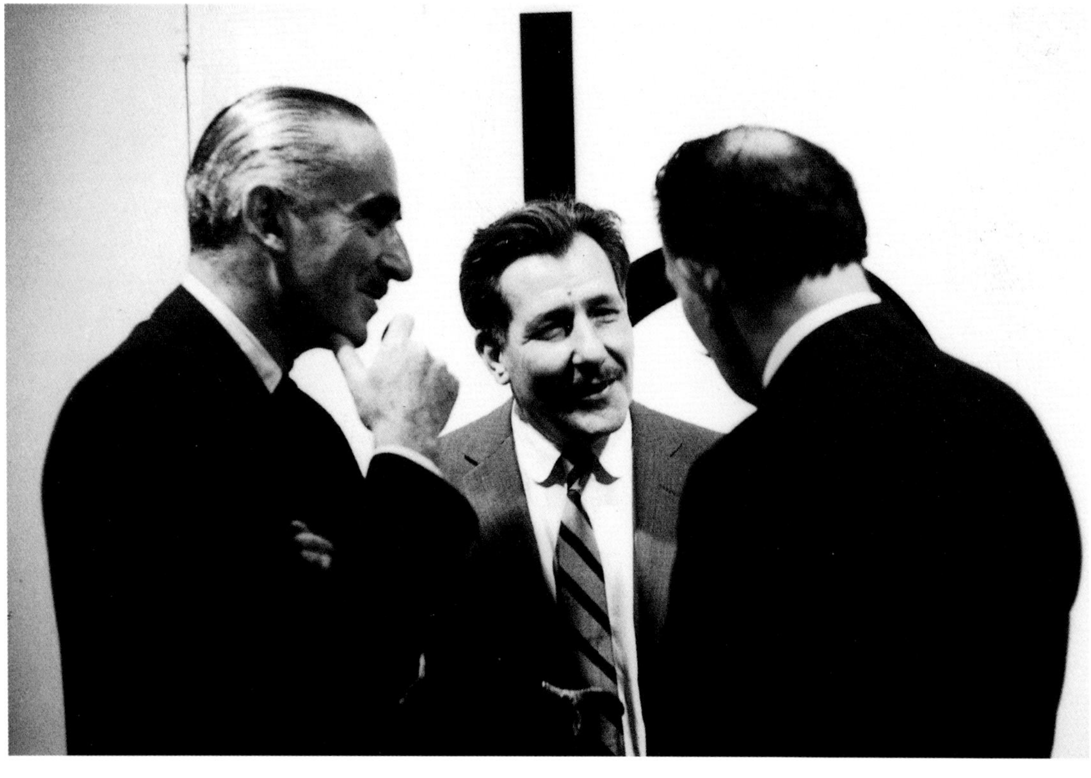

Betty Parsons (top) and Franz Kline (bottom).

"You weren't supposed to have both Condé Nast and Betty Parsons in the art world of 1960," Kazanjian and Tomkins wrote, addressing the "sulfurous whiff of contempt for the marriage of art and fashion." The other mythic figure at *Vogue*, Diana Vreeland, announced on seeing his paintings, "Oh Alex they'd make such beautiful sweaters!"

"Alex and I like to think we have nothing to do with fashion," wrote Irving Penn. In fact, the paintings have nothing to do with what was fashionable at the time. Liberman predicted Minimalism by a decade. Abstract Expressionism was the "game" at the Parsons gallery and Pop Art was emerging from the very magazine pages Liberman edited. But it was the perception of Alex's life in the fashion world that distanced his work from a certain critical and popular success. How could he be serious? How could the paintings be serious?

These seem to be naive questions in our Murakami obsessed Louis Vuitton society where Armani walks on the Guggenheim "runway." To be friends with Marlene Dietrich and Babe Paley would be a badge of honor to an artist today. It must have seemed naive to Liberman whose life in Europe saw the mingling of art forms everywhere from fashion – Schiaparelli and Dalí, Cocteau, and Man Ray – to journalism. He could do both and saw no reason not to. There was no need to lead the clichéd life of artistic poverty. Nor did he see a contradiction in his two roles. Art and life were not separate.

Today art and fashion coexist in worlds of high and low art. Amy Gross, a colleague at Condé Nast, best summarized Liberman's insatiable need to create when she said, "You either go high or low, but you don't muck around in the middle, because it's boring and banal." There was certainly nothing boring or banal about Liberman's life or work.

for Melinda
W.A.
January 2004

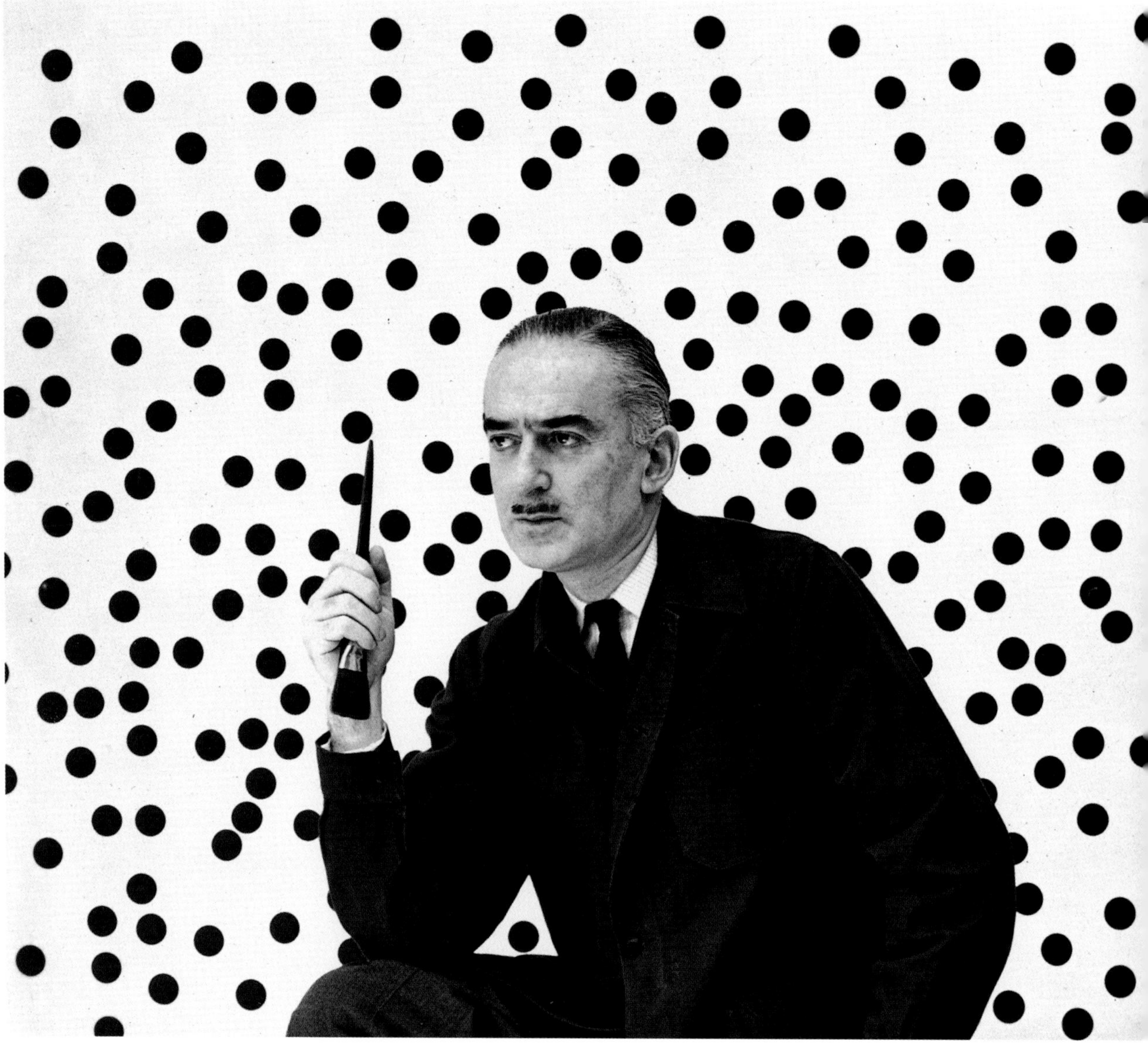

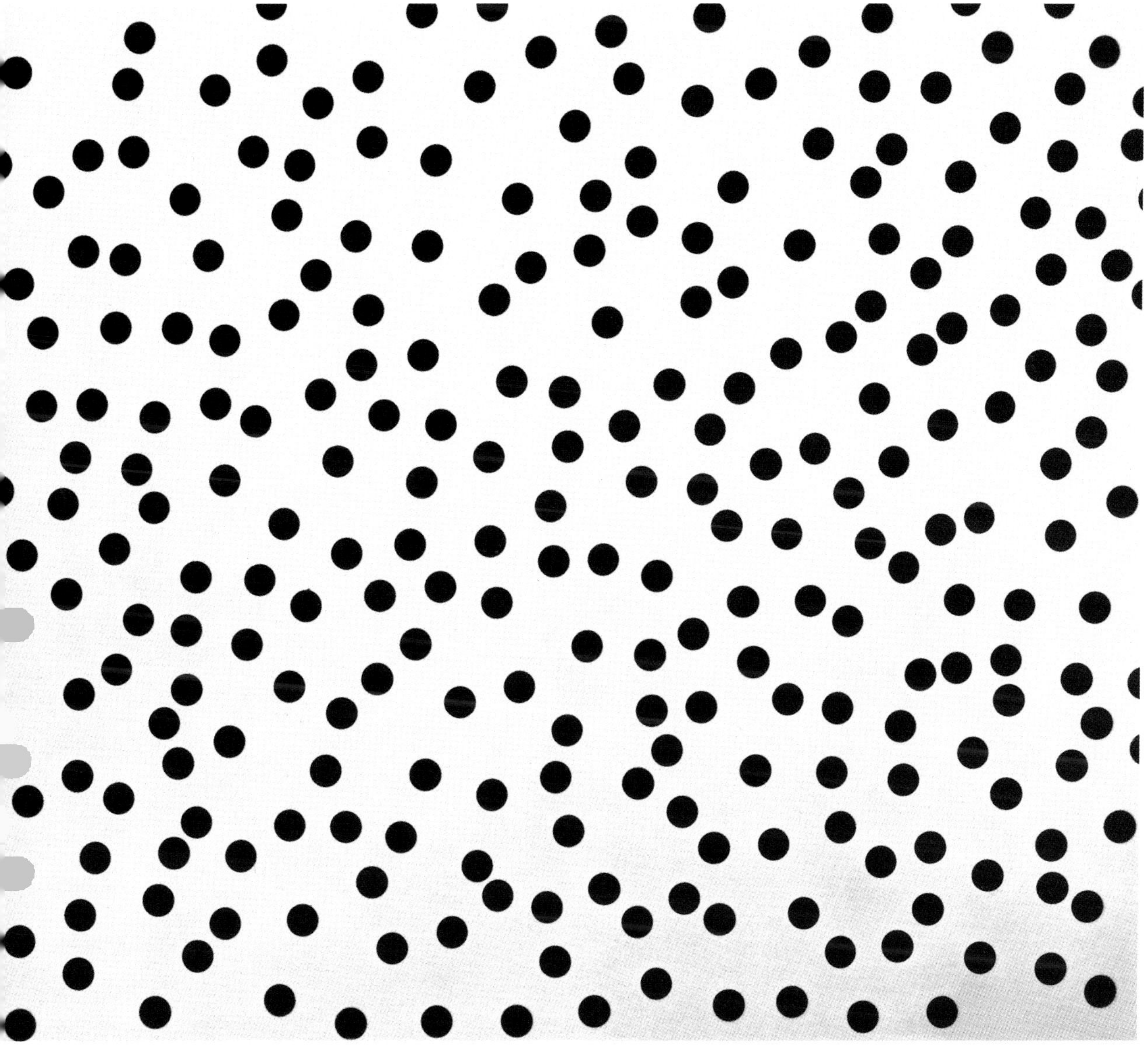

catalogue of the exhibition

Four Hundred Plus
1959, acrylic on canvas
40 x 82 inches, 101.6 x 208.3 cm

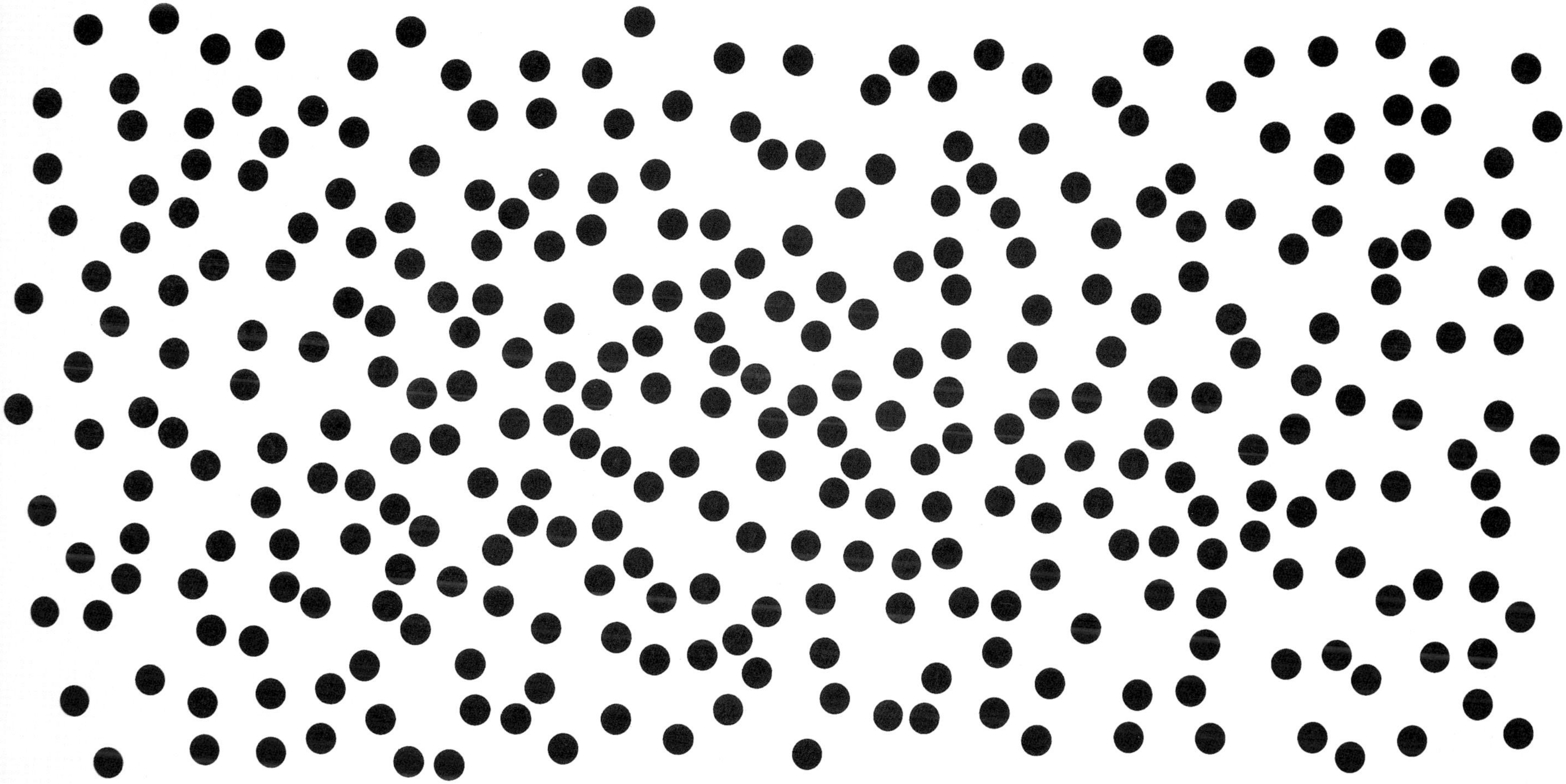

Diptych – One Way
1950, oil and enamel on masonite
60 x 74¼ inches, 152.4 x 188.6 cm

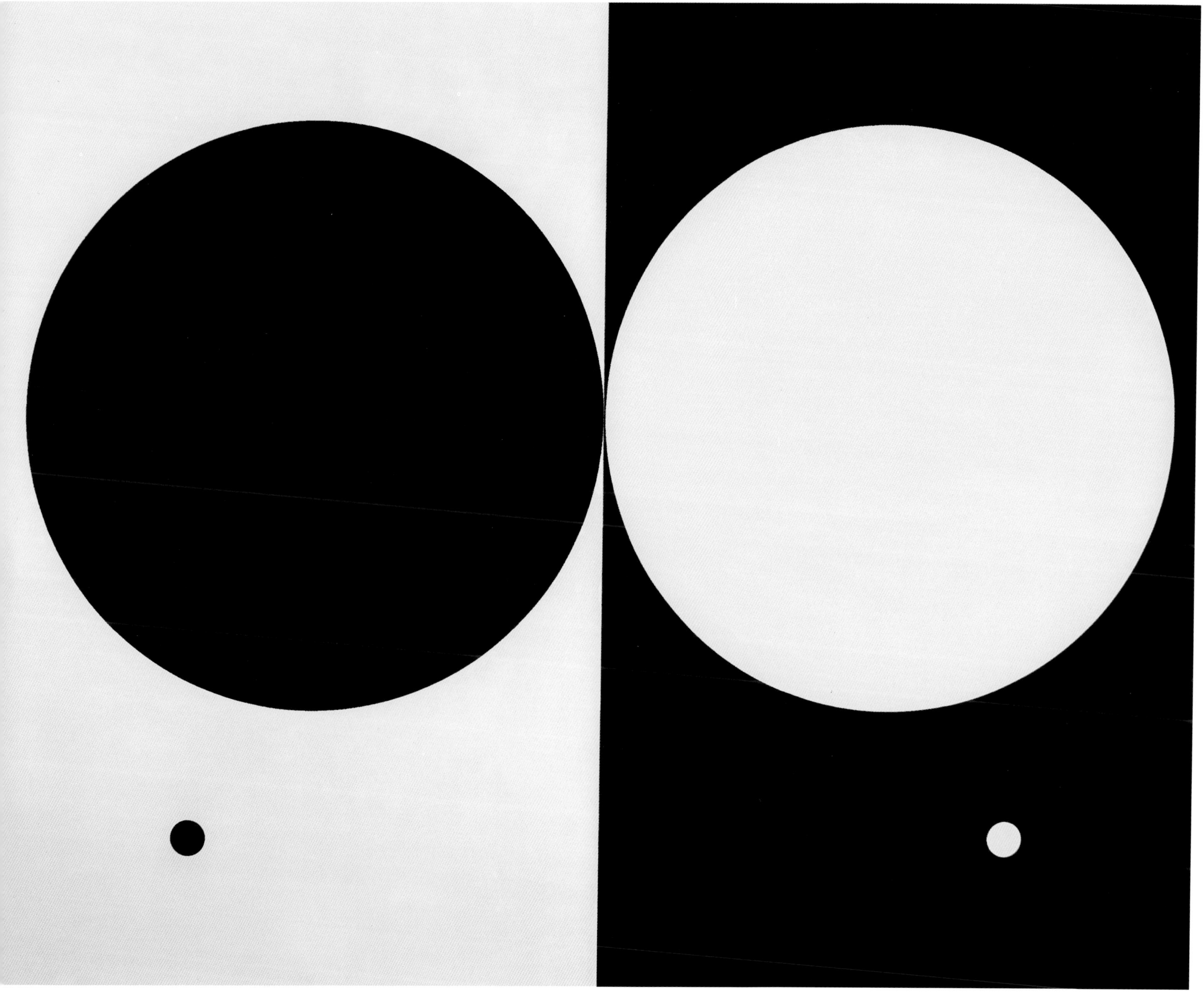

Diptych – Two Ways
1950, oil and enamel on masonite
60 x 74¼ inches, 152.4 x 188.6 cm

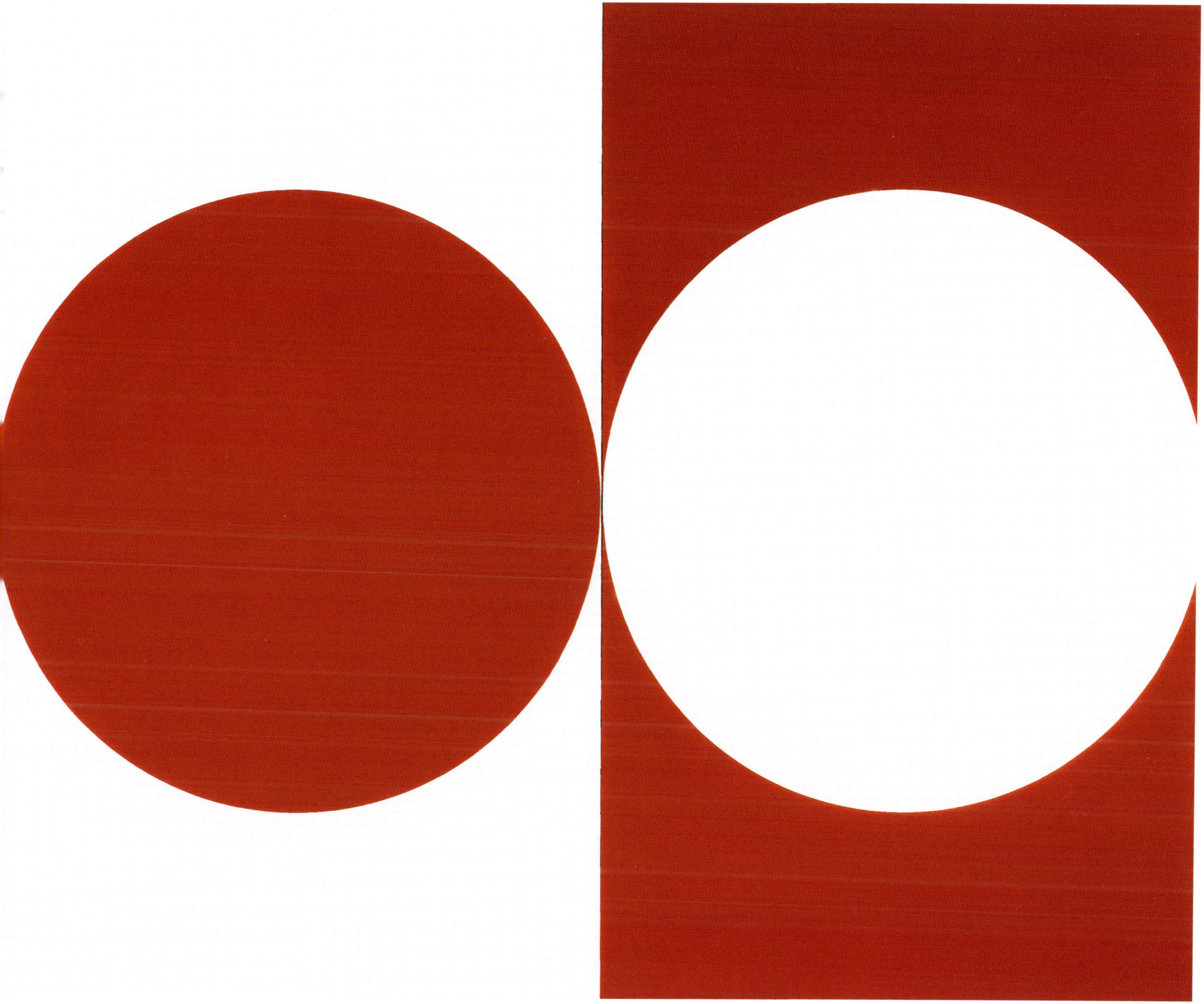

Untitled
n.d., oil on canvas
18 x 24 inches, 45.7 x 61 cm

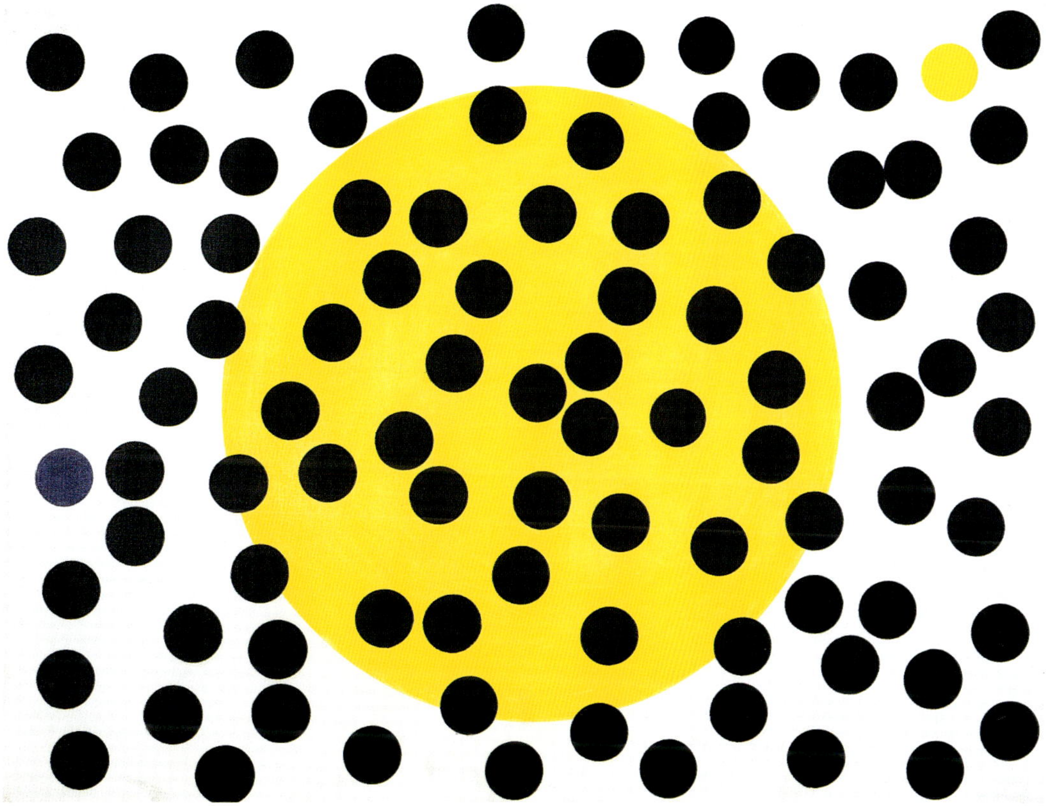

Untitled
n.d., oil on canvas
20 x 24$\frac{1}{8}$ inches, 50.8 x 61.3 cm

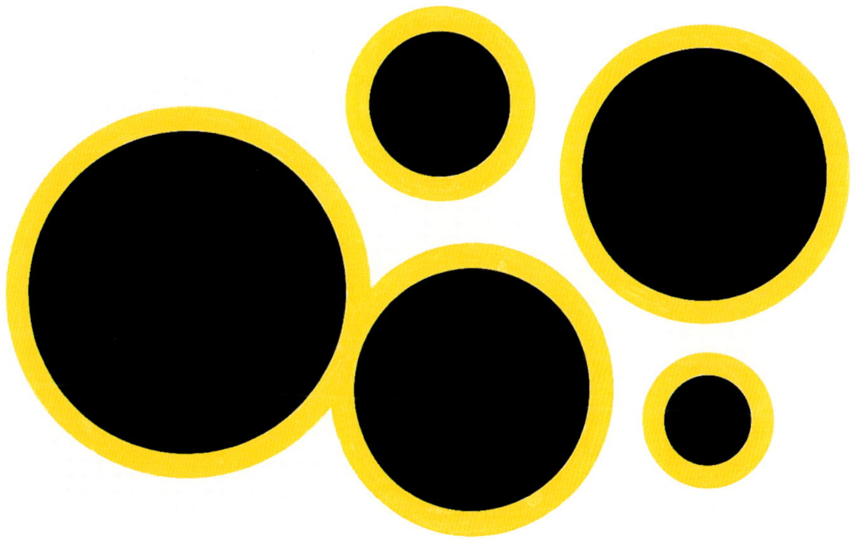

Untitled
1955, enamel on masonite
48 x 96 inches, 121.9 x 243.8 cm

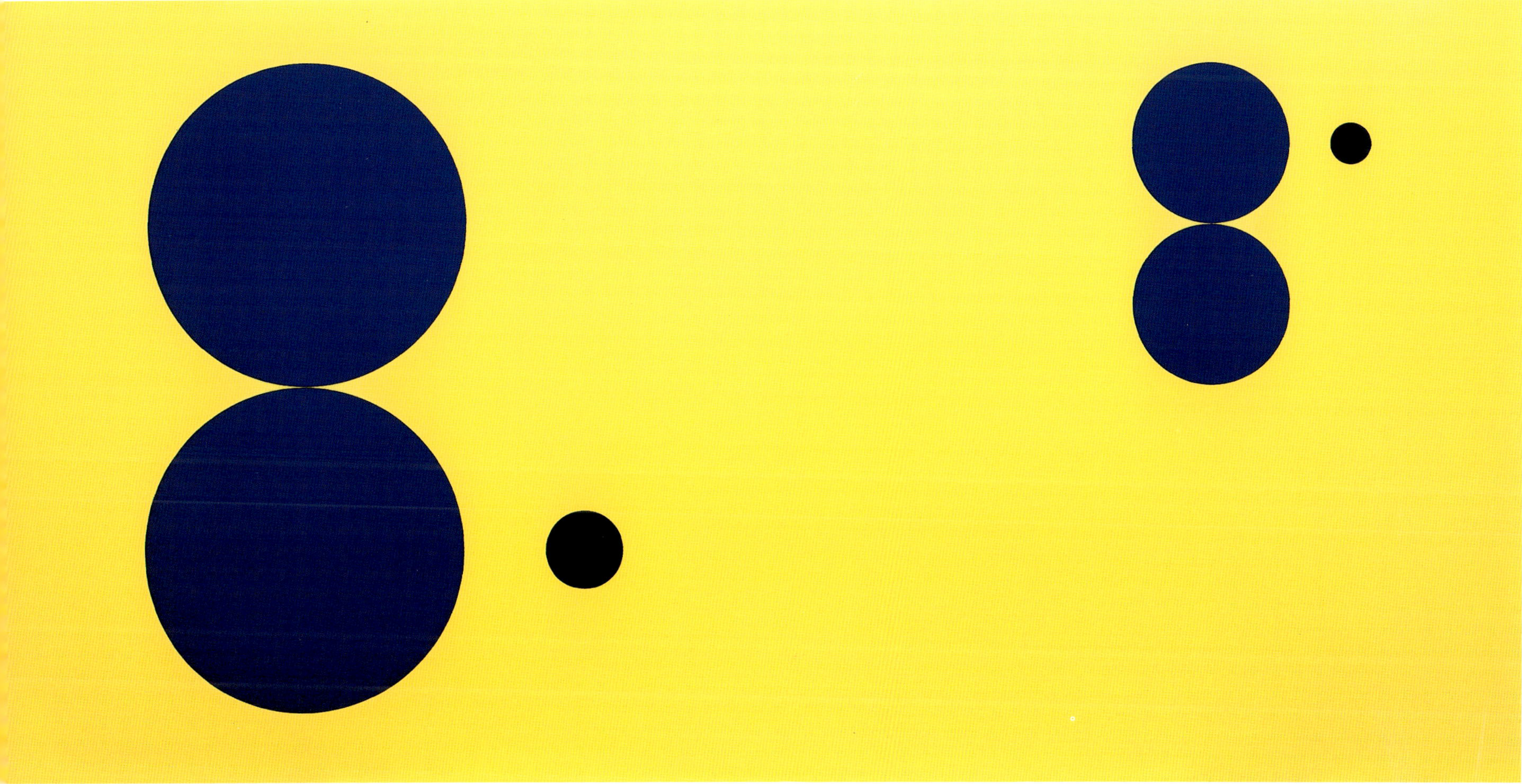

Untitled
1955, oil on canvas
40 x 50 inches, 101.6 x 127 cm

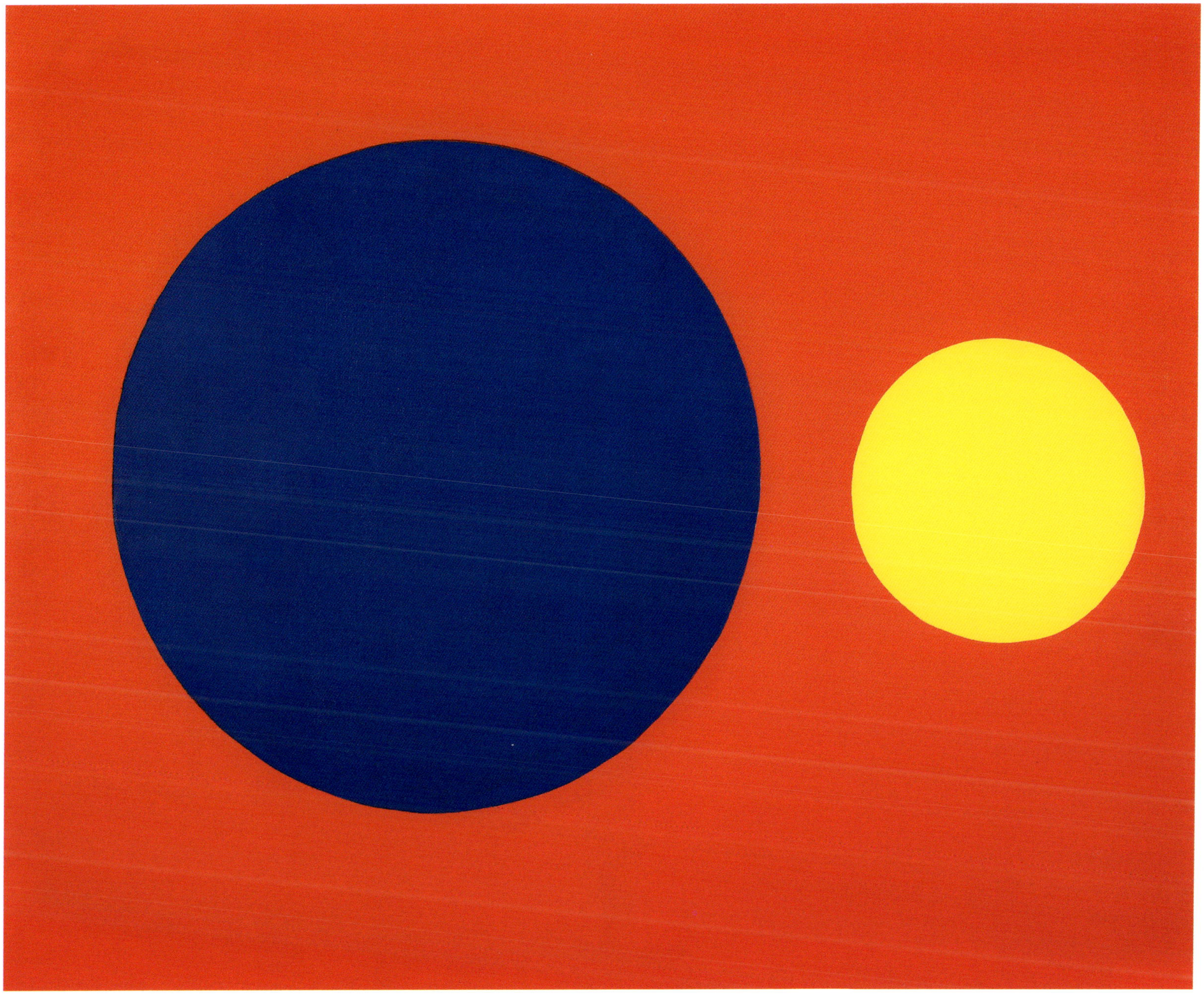

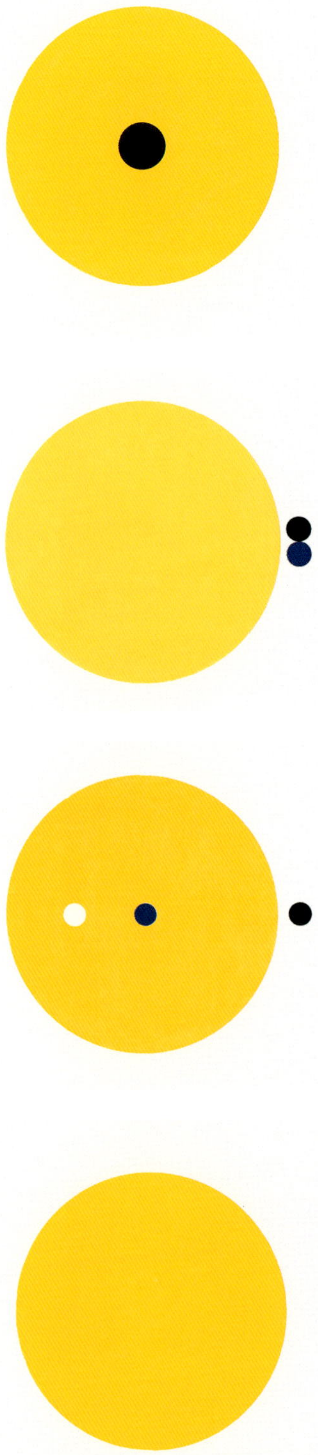

Yellow Continuum
1958-59, oil on canvas
20 x 24¼ inches, 50.8 x 61.6 cm

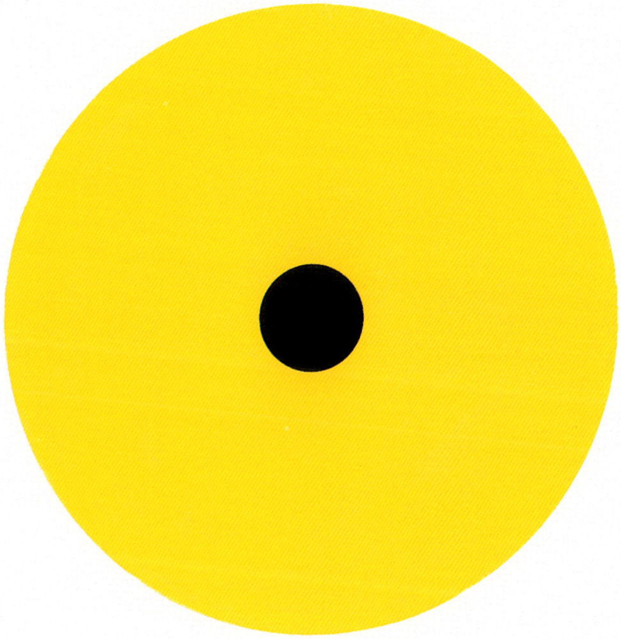

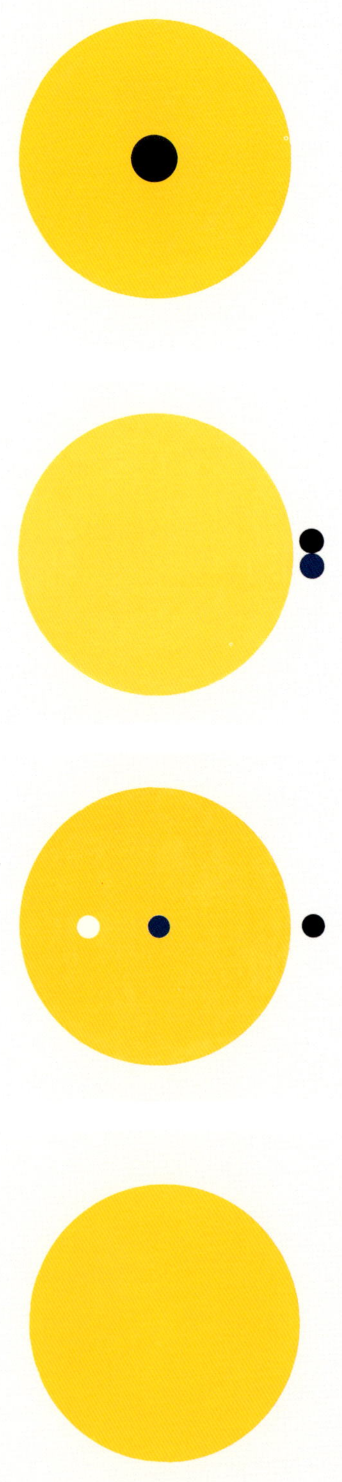

Yellow Continuum
1958-59, oil on canvas
18 x 20 inches, 45.7 x 50.8 cm

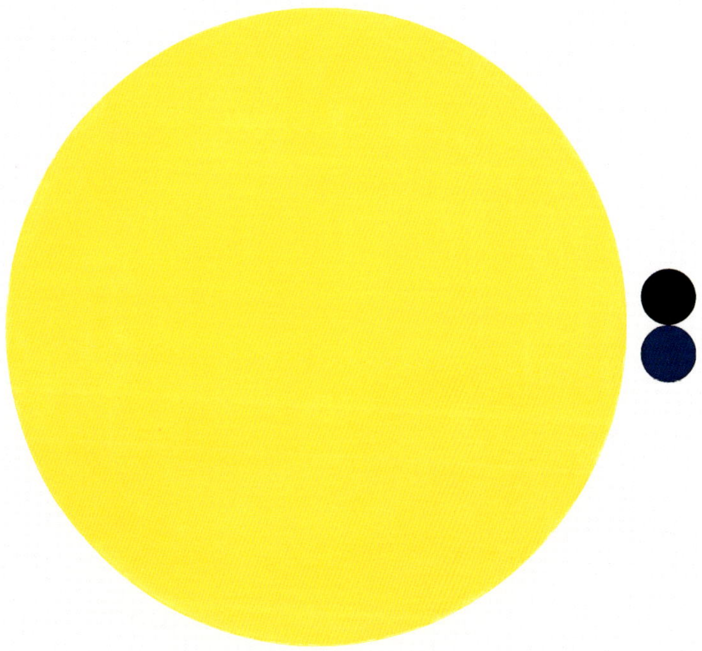

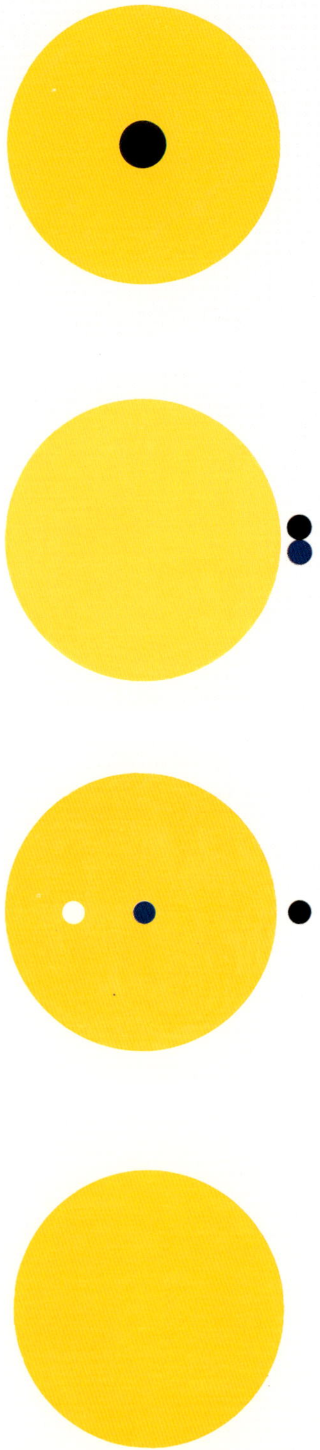

Yellow Continuum
1958-59, oil on canvas
18 x 20 inches, 45.7 x 50.8 cm

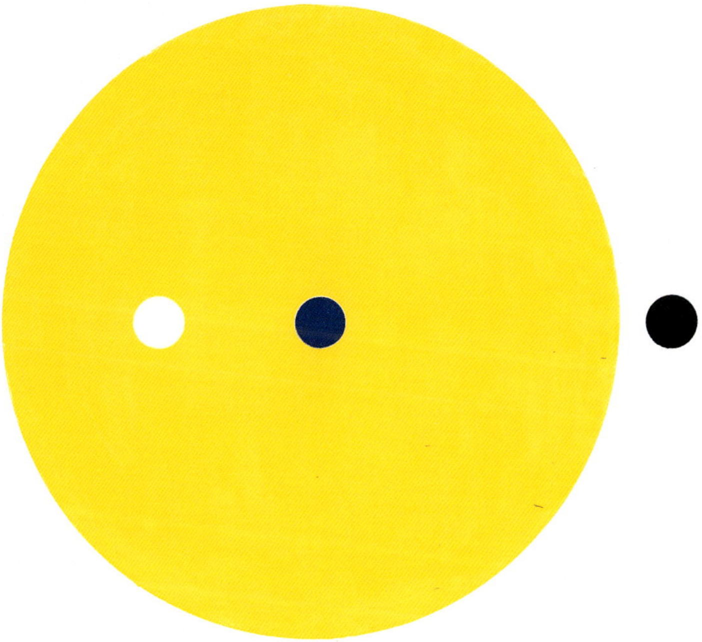

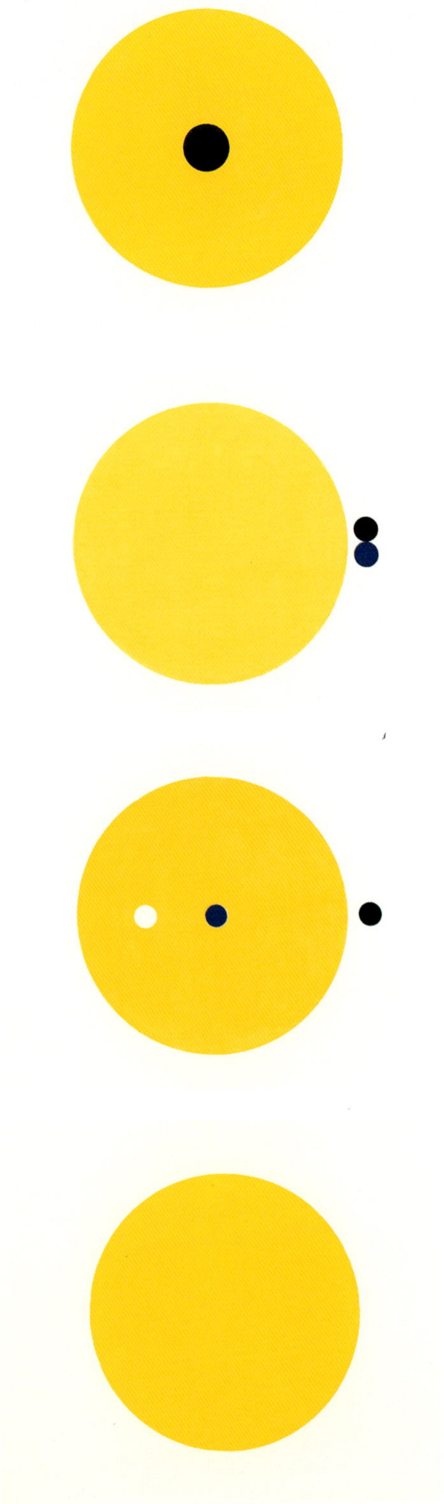

Yellow Continuum
1958-59, oil on canvas
20 x 24¼ inches, 50.8 x 61.6 cm

Blue Opposite Red
1959, oil on canvas
40 x 82 inches, 101.6 x 208.3 cm

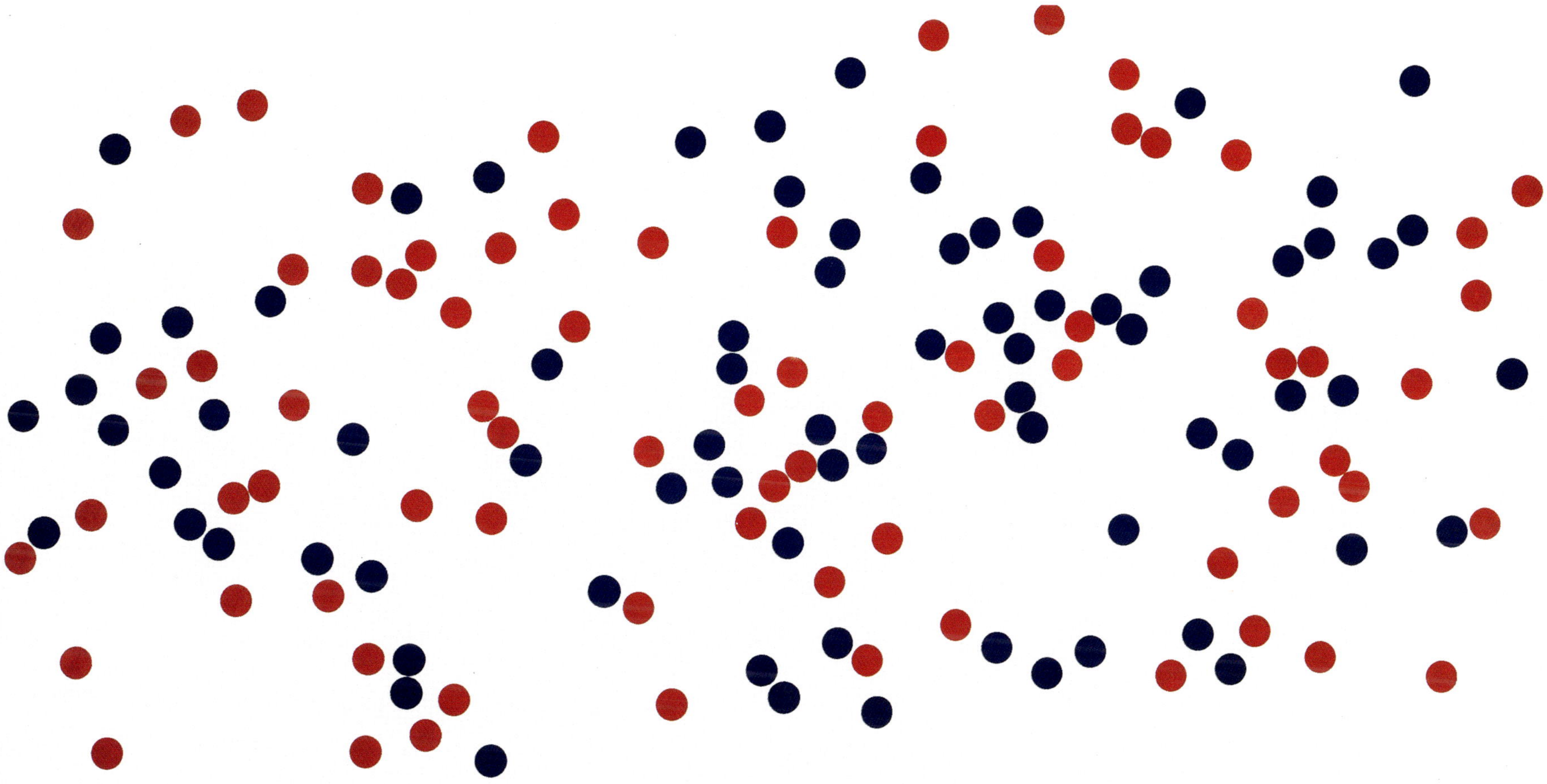

Untitled
1959, acrylic on canvas
24 x 36 inches, 61 x 91.4 cm

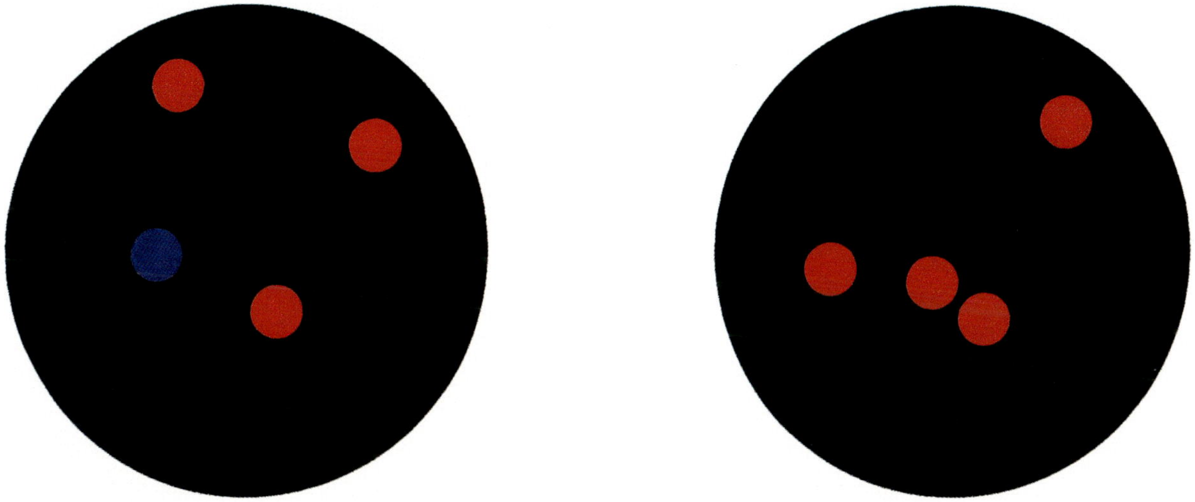

Repetition
1959, oil on canvas
30 x 36 inches, 76.2 x 91.4 cm

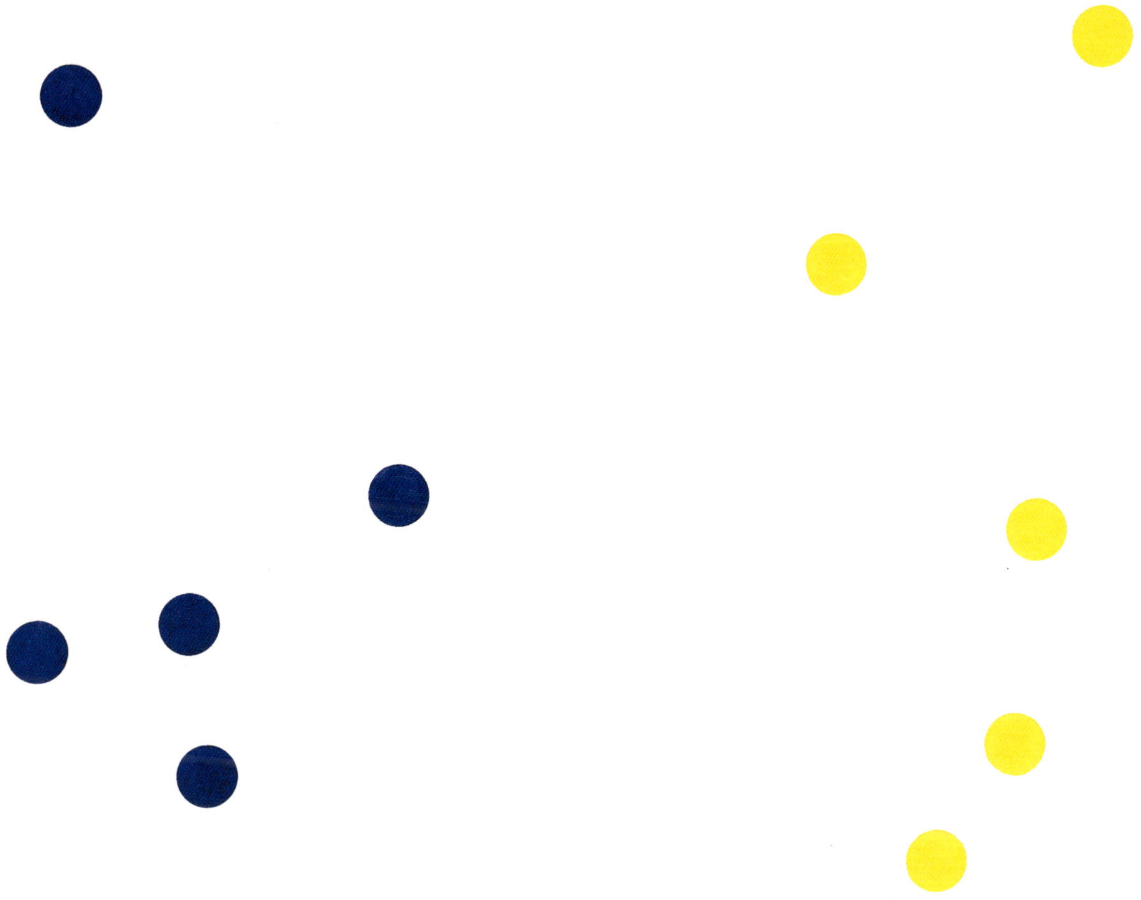

Black End
1959, oil on canvas
24 x 36 inches, 61 x 91.4 cm

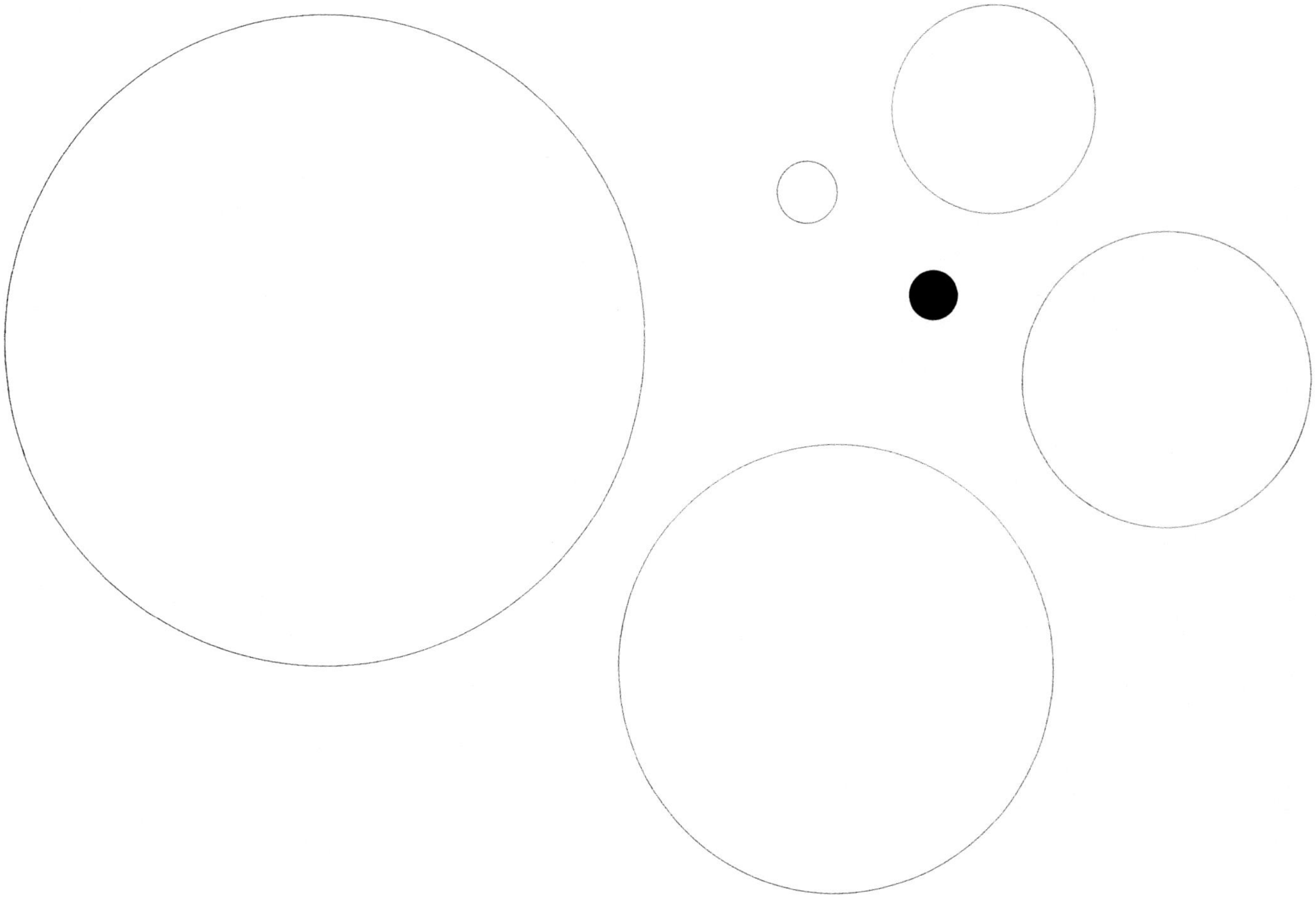

Untitled
1960, oil on canvas
30 x 40 inches, 76.2 x 101.6 cm

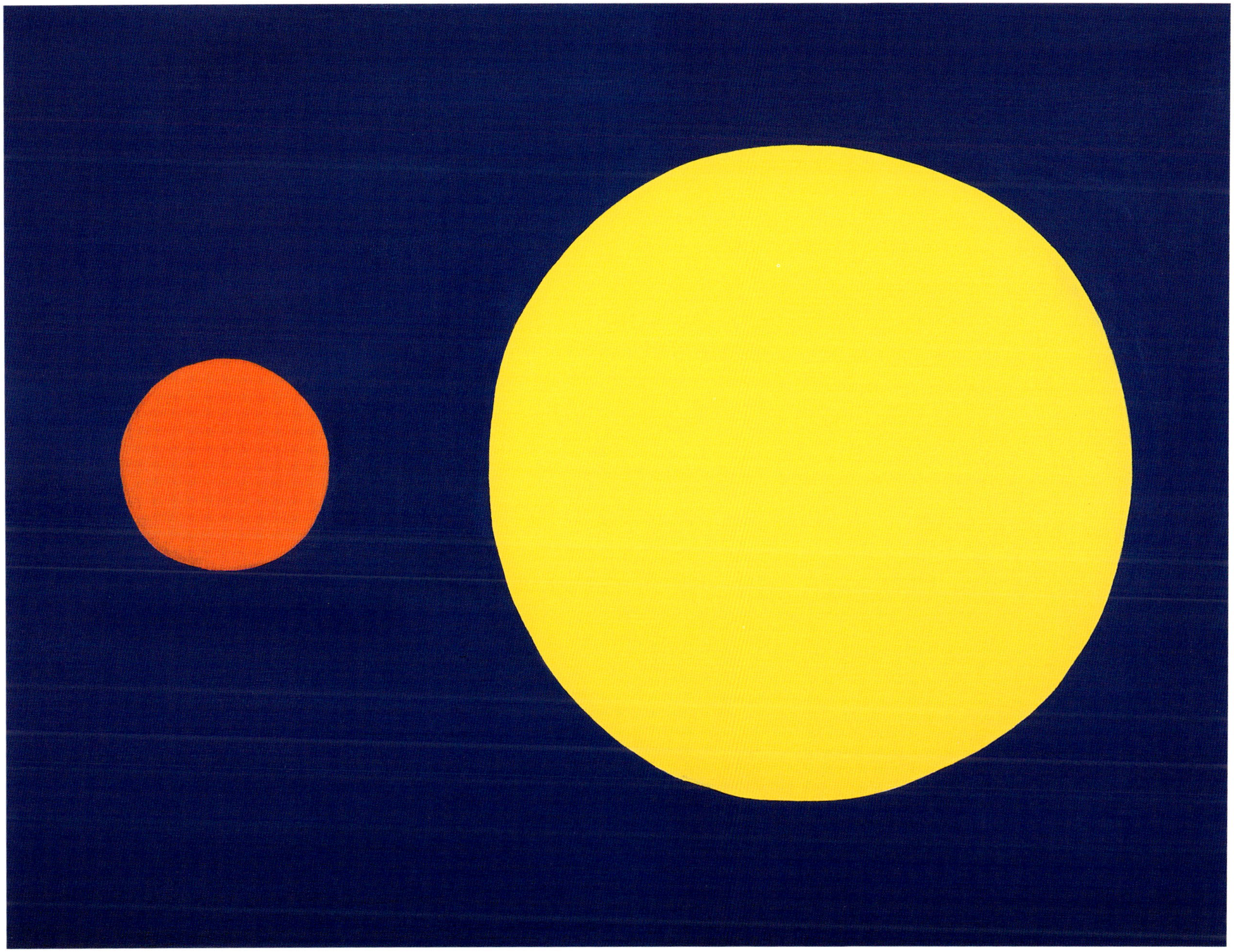

Alexander Liberman began to paint circles in 1950; he pursued the concept for thirteen years with an intensity that is felt like a cutting edge beneath the pictures' burnished surfaces.

They seemed merely geometric or outlandish in the early fifties, at the peak moment in Abstract Expressionism's gestural phase. Nowadays, hindsight clarifies the presence of a strong will to impersonal, cool, almost invisible structures that ran parallel to the famous sweeping gestures and dripping impastos. Barnett Newman found and made explicit the vertical, dividing shape; Liberman chose the circle; both were passionately involved in symmetrical formats, simple color sensations, the resources of white and, especially, black. And the difference between, say, the roiled paint of a Willem de Kooning or a Franz Kline and Newman's or Liberman's sleek presentations could be called "violently superficial;" they shared intentions more crucial than any cosmetic appearance.

For all the major New York artists, the issue was to crack the brittle deposits of style that had encrusted modern art, and to find a sensation of reality that would be tangible, literal, "there." All of them wanted to jettison the protocols of composition and pictorial mechanics in order to define an image that could be grasped all at once, whole – self-evident. And all of them sought to incorporate chance – hazard, the aleatory, spontaneity – into the work, not as another technique (which the Surrealists had done), but as an organic part of the picture, penetrating form and content equally.

The particularity of Liberman's move — you could call it a "leap," for he had been dedicated to painterly, abstract syntheses from nature — was in how he ordered his procedures. Luck, chance, the unforeseeable, came first. Instead of locating its analogue in accidents on the surface of wet paint — in drips, swipes, happy blots — Liberman invoked the unexpected at the planning stage. He threw dice, tossed poker chips, invoked *I Ching* rituals of change, to establish the format according to certain very general rules. When satisfied with the results, or suitably dissatisfied, or astonished, he executed the painting with a maximum of precision and a minimum of interference or temperament. Sometimes he would send the picture out to be fabricated according to his exact specifications. Often he adopted "advanced" materials and technologies (he had, he remembers, a European's awe of American corporate know-how; "if you want a white," he decided, "why not use the stuff they put on the doors of refrigerators?" — this was before the days we knew about built-in obsolescence).

The result is an extraordinary object that, in theory, presents an accident that was planned to happen, and then planned to be recorded with calculating accuracy — an aleatory glimpse trapped in the clearest of crystals. Art, however, is predictable only for its elusions of theory. The work keeps slipping from the grasp of the worker. It warps in response to certain interior pressures that correspond to interior demands in the artist himself, even though he has sternly banished them from the studio. The absence of the hand-made look quickly becomes another, only-slightly-different autograph. The friction along the double helix that gets Marilyn Monroe from a rainbow trout (I don't vouch for this evolutionary ladder) also changes a circle from an abstract shape aspiring to some metaphysical incarnation into the idiosyncratic Liberman circle. His fingerprint. I'm sure that the future art historians will find it a striking self-portrait.

Not that Liberman's circles ever were Platonic sunbathers dreaming of *pi*. As he developed the theme, it conflated private, mythologizing agents, like lightning to primitive man. A circle is the iris of the eye, the primal void, the equator (and thus a perfectly straight line laid flat on the picture plane) a cylinder pushing in, a tunnel, a disc (Yin, Aton), that coincidental triad with framing verticals which, in san-serif type, spells **g o d.**

There no longer should be any real surprise in this. We have discovered poetic, often religious, substructures in almost all modern abstract art. Liberman's circles no more aspire to a purity of line, color, and form than do Mondrian's right angles, Newman's meticulous "zips," or Pollock's weaving throws of paint. The surprise in Liberman's circle paintings is that, in spite of their intimate ties to the intellectual matrix of the 1950's, they also predict so much of the style of the 1960's. The target shape (a trademark of New York painting, 1959-64) is introduced; so are the dancing after-images (in a number of pictures, Liberman carefully choreographed them for symmetrical drills). The large-scale uncomposed, flat, smooth, sharp-edged, intense-hued, wholistic painting that offers itself to the viewer without explanations is foretold in this oeuvre.

It's typical of Liberman (and typical of the best American artists) that he abandoned the vein just as it was becoming fashionable. He would have moved on anyhow. He was hungry for paint. Also, he preserved the circle motif in giant sculptures with rings and sliced cylinders which still are in progress.

The one sadly astonishing thing is that this obsessional art – so much a piece of our tradition – is still so little known.

—Thomas B. Hess, 1974

Alexander Liberman, Edward Steichen and an unidentified woman at the opening of Liberman's 1959 Museum of Modern Art exhibition ***The Artist in His Studio***.

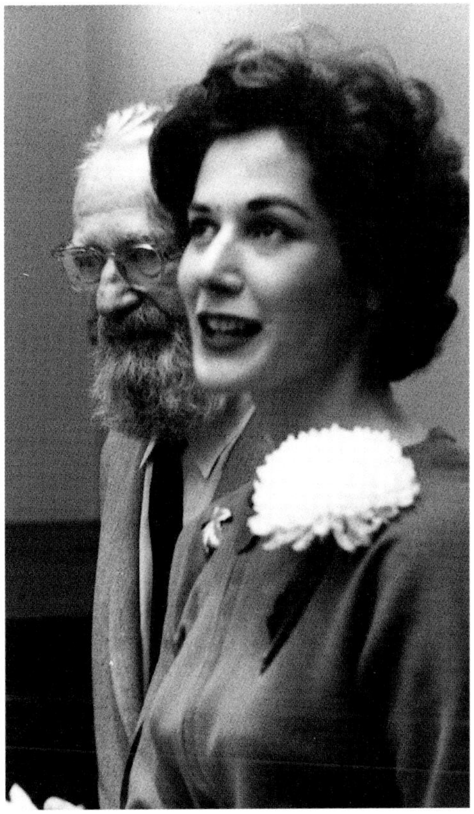
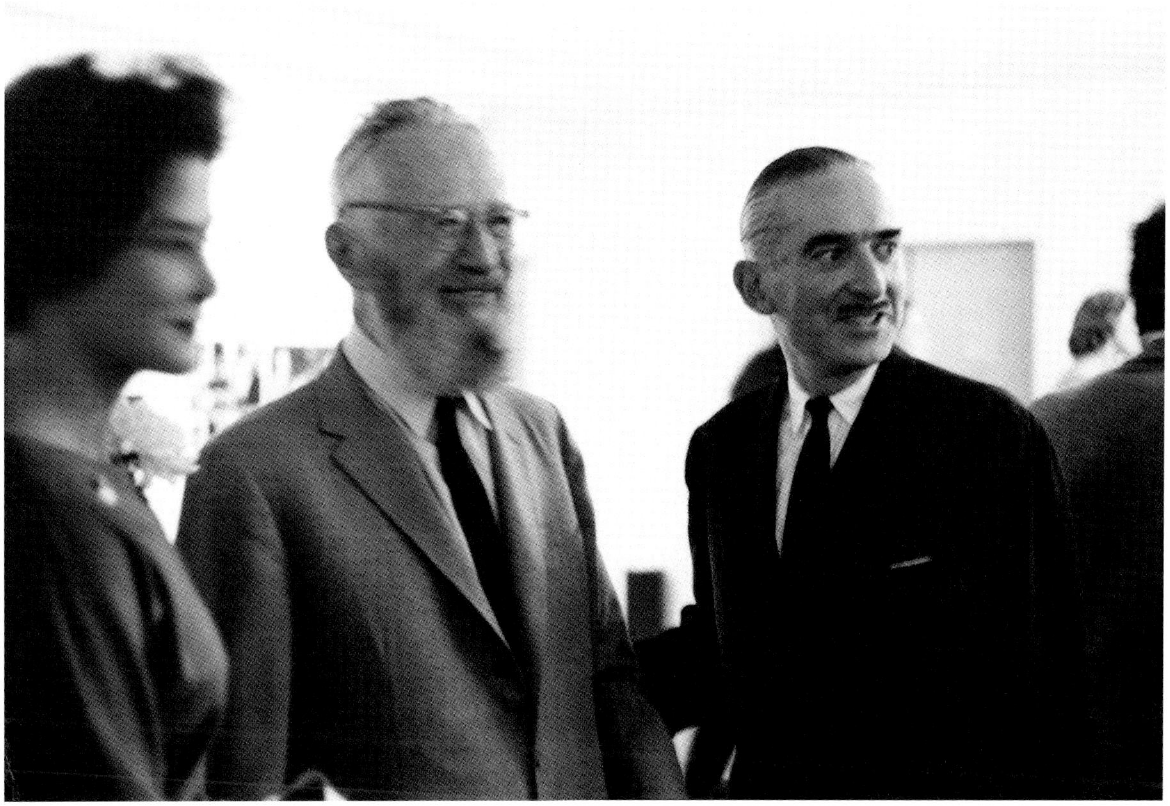
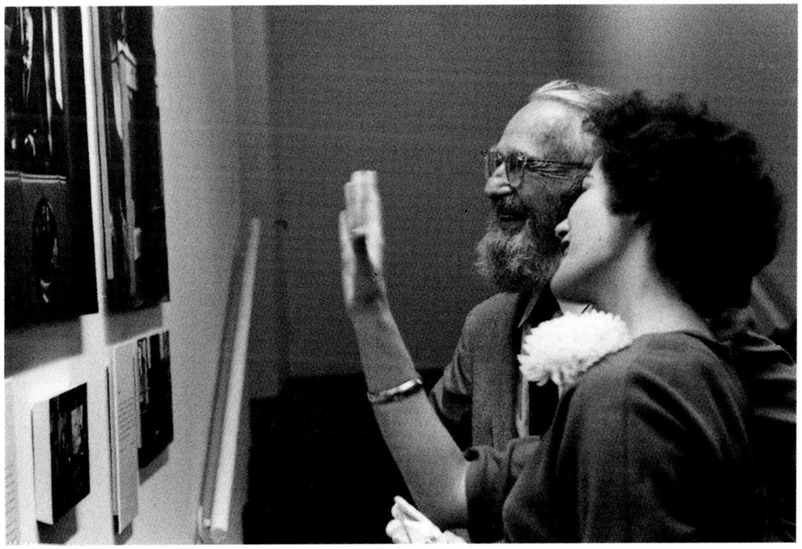
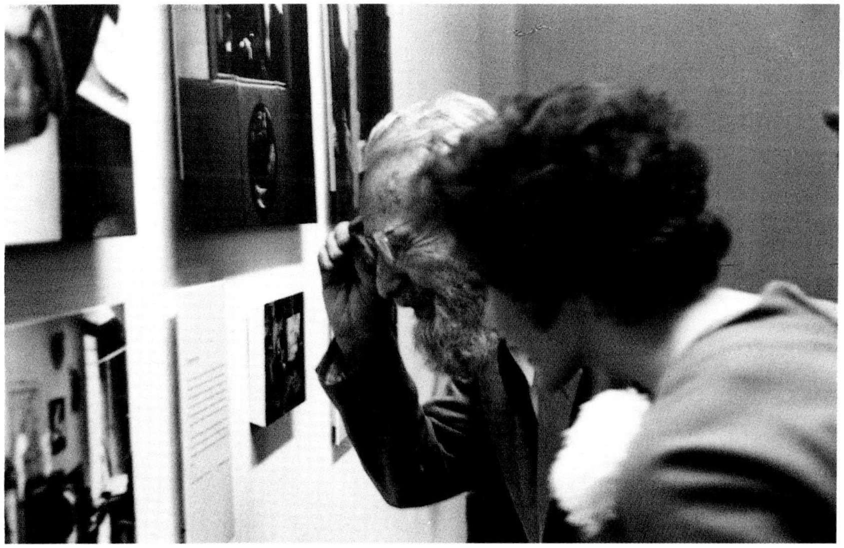

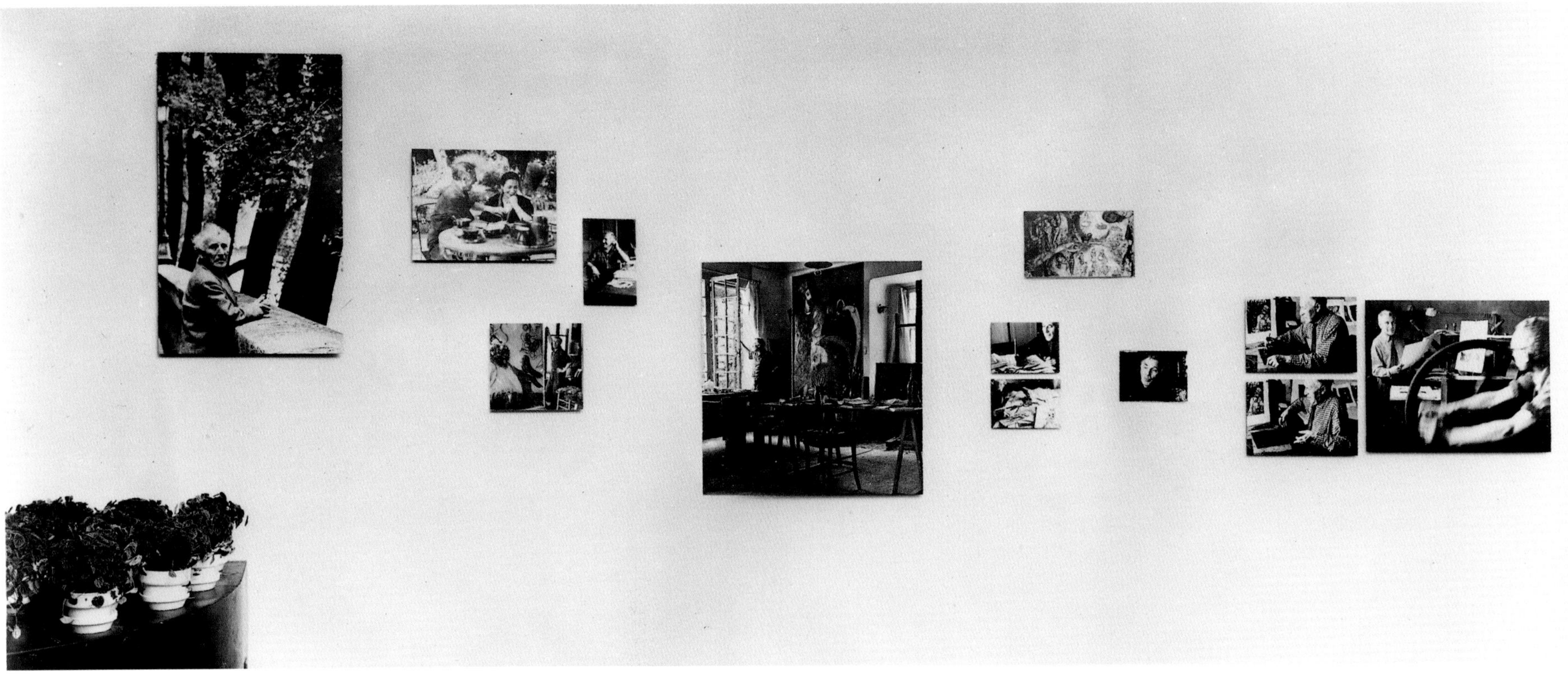

Installation photograph from ***The Artist in His Studio*** (featuring Marc Chagall above and Alberto Giacometti opposite).

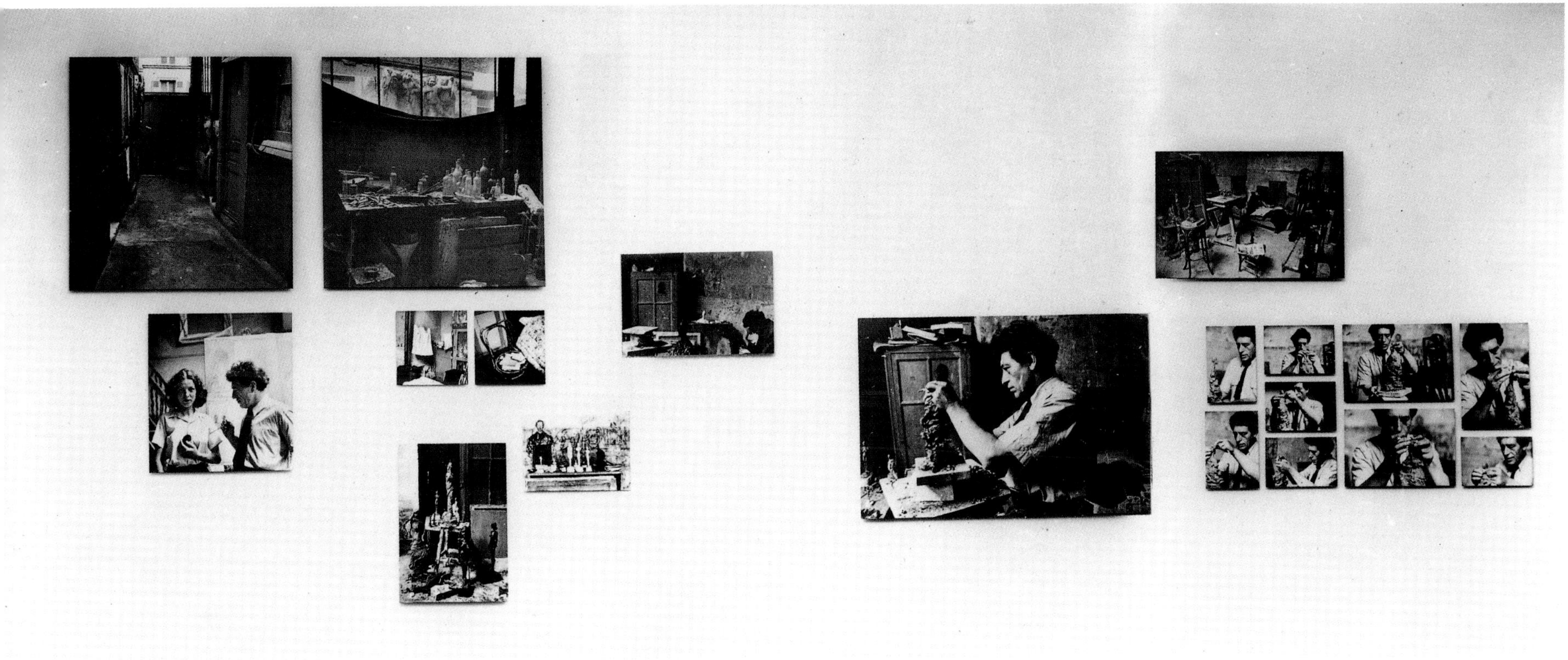

The economy is admirable.

— Donald Judd

Arts April 1960

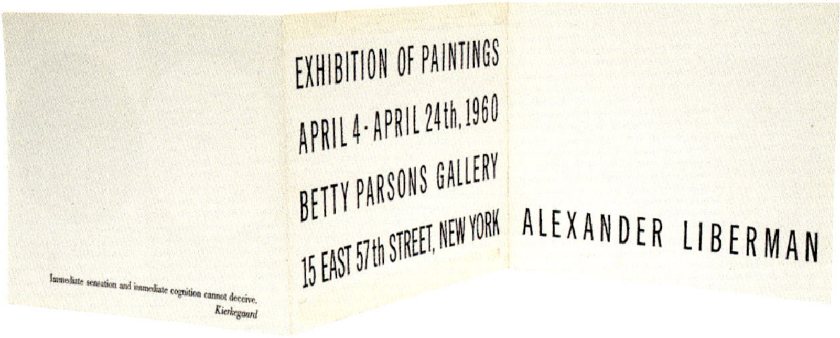

Exhibition announcement design by Alexander Liberman, 1960

Published on the occasion of the exhibition

Alexander Liberman
No Regrets

25 March – 24 April 2004

Ameringer & Yohe Fine Art
20 West 57th Street
New York, New York 10019
tel: 212 445 0051 fax: 212 445 0051

Color transparencies by Jordan Tinker

With special thanks to André Emmerich for his kind permission
to reprint the Thomas B. Hess essay from his exhibition catalogue,
Alexander Liberman: The Circle Paintings 1950-1964
(October 5 – October 23, 1974).

Catalogue designed by HHA Design, New York with Will Ameringer
Printed by Paola Gribaudo, Torino, Italy

ISBN: 0-9719796-9-3

AMERINGER
YOHE
FINE ART

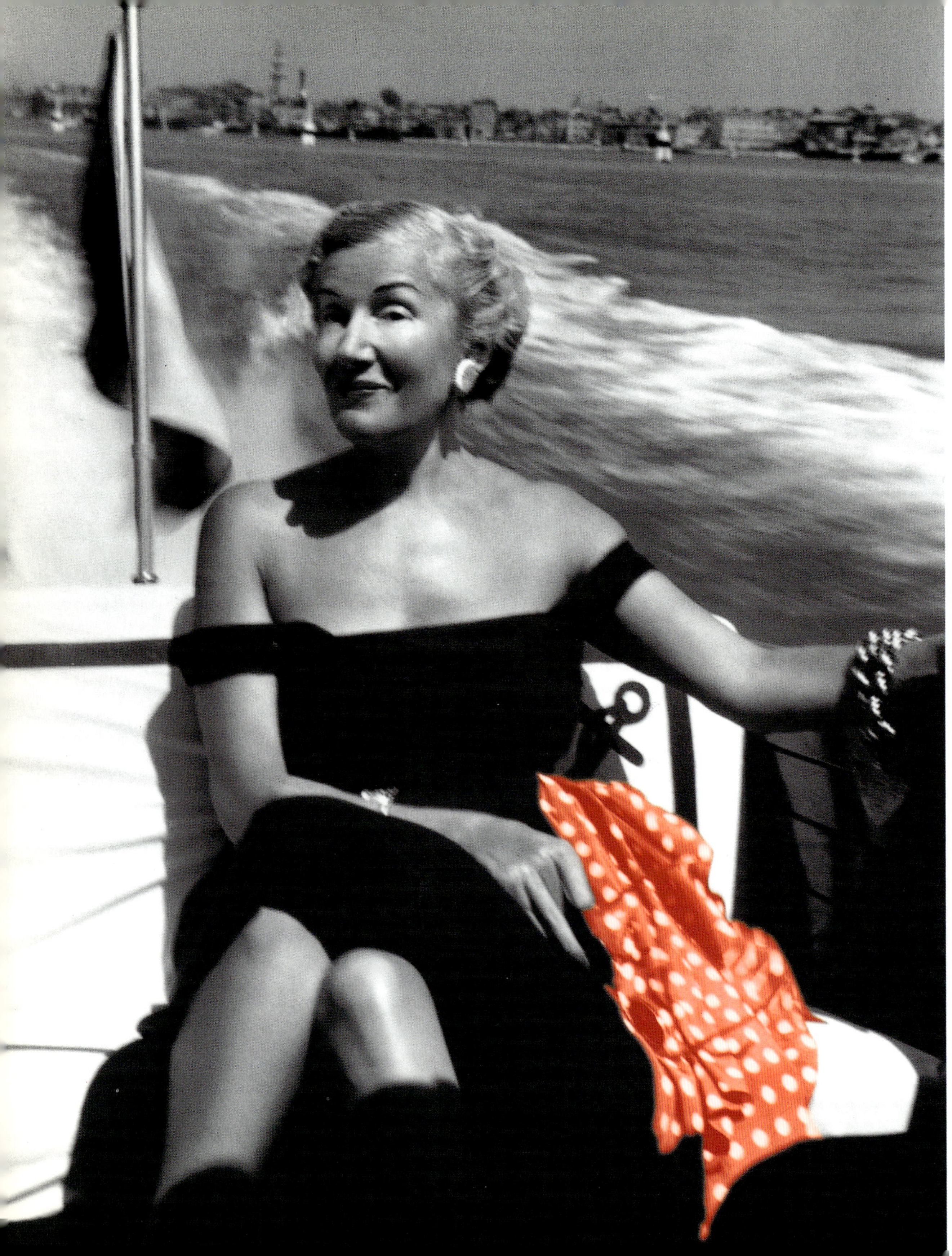

"Alex is superman"
— Tatiana